# The Funky Piglets
# Volume 1

Richard Mark Smith
Illustrated by Ashley Hipperson

The Funky Piglets, Volume 1

Copyright © 2015, Richard Mark Smith

All rights reserved.

No part of this book may be reproduced by any means, nor transmitted, nor translated into a machine language, without the written permission of the publishers.

Condition of Sale

This book is sold subject to the condition that it shall not, by way of trade or otherwise, be lent, re-sold, hired out or otherwise circulated in any form of binding or cover other than that in which it is published and without a similar condition including this condition being imposed on the subsequent purchaser.

Disclaimer

This book is a work of fiction. Names, places, characters, and events are the product of the author's imagination. Any resemblance to actual persons, living or dead, events, or locales is purely coincidental.

Dedicated to
Rachel, Charlie, George and Anna.

# GHOSTIES

There are ghosties in my bedroom
and ghosties in my hall.
All night they try to frighten me
by banging on the wall.

Then as the clock strikes midnight
they float around and shout,
"This house does not belong to you.
GET OUT! GET OUT! GET OUT!"

But what those spooks don't realise,
as they bang and scream and yell,
is I am not afraid of them
'cos I'm a ghost as well!

# THE RED-EYED MONSTER

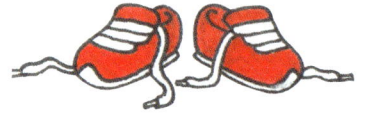

The red-eyed monster stomps around.
Her rumbly tum makes a gurgling sound.
She's frantically searching for her tea.
Oh no! Look out! She's eating ...

The Funky Piglets, Volume 1

# SPOOKY
# TREE

Outside my bedroom window
there lives a spooky tree.
As soon as I climb into bed
it leans and watches me.

Then every night at midnight,
as clouds conceal the moon,
it climbs in through my window
and looks around my room!

It takes my toys and teddy bears
and then, without a sound,
jumps swiftly out the window
and back into the ground.

I do not like the spooky tree.
It's nasty, mean and frightening.
And so I pray one stormy day
this tree gets struck by lightning!

# TIME TO MOVE OUT

Daddy cooks my breakfast.
Mummy cooks my tea.
They wash my clothes, make my bed
and clean up after me.

# The Funky Piglets, Volume 1

They even brush my teeth at night.
I think it's really cool.
The only thing I have to do
is eat and go to school.

But Mummy said I must move out.
 The reason, as you'll see,
  is I'm the school's headmaster
   and I'll soon be sixty-three!

# SIDNEY THE SPARROW

Young Sidney the sparrow was learning to fly, but he couldn't take off so he started to cry. He practised for hours but, try as he might, the poor little birdie just couldn't take flight.

## The Funky Piglets, Volume 1

So he said to his grandpa,
"Oh what shall I do?
I feel like my poor wings
are covered in glue!"
But Grandpops just smiled as he
pulled from his pocket
the key to his shed that
contained a large rocket.

Poor Sidney looked frightened
and tried hard to muster
some courage as Grandpa strapped
on the large thruster.
"You ready to fly, boy?"
Gramps said with a grin
as he lit the touch-paper,
then dived in the bin!

The rocket went *BOOM!*,
blasting Sid through the sky.
He cried with delight as at
last he could fly.
Now Sidney's so fast that a
squadron of sparrows
have made him team leader
of the famous Red Arrows!

# SADNESS

Today I feel like crying.
Today I'm feeling sad.
I've just been very naughty
and told off by my dad.

The Funky Piglets, Volume 1

My mum is also cross with me.
"Straight to your room!" she said.
So I'm going to find my teddy bear
and spend the day in bed.

# I WANT TO BE A FAIRY!

I want to be a fairy
in the Christmas play,
but when I told Miss Pringle
she didn't know what to say.

The Funky Piglets, Volume 1

She paused a while and then replied,
"Perhaps you could play Mary."
So I jumped upon her desk and screamed,
"I WANT TO BE A FAIRY!"

And so for being rude to her
Miss Pringle made me pay ...
by making me the donkey
in our high-school Christmas play!

# RABBIT PIE?

A cunning young fox
wearing bright-purple socks
was chillaxing under a tree.
She saw a small rabbit
and thought, "I must grab it
to make a nice pie for my tea."

 The Funky Piglets, Volume 1

But the cute little bunny
thought something was funny
so, wiping the sweat from his head,
he grabbed hold of the fox
and her bright-purple socks
and made vixen hot-pot instead!

# YOU CAN'T FOOL MUM

I want to spend the day in bed
so from my pencil case,
I took a bright-red marker pen
and squished spots on my face.

The Funky Piglets, Volume 1

I said to Mum, "I don't feel well,"
then showed her all my spots.
I told her I had measles, mumps,
the flu and chickenpox.

But Mum just took one look at me
and said, "I'm not a fool!"
then grabbed my bright-red marker pen
and screamed out, "GET TO SCHOOL!"

# MY YUCKY BROTHER!

My yucky little brother
squishes worms and bugs!
He eats the bogeys from his nose
and earwax from his lugs.

The Funky Piglets, Volume 1

He dribbles on the toilet seat
and plays with slimy frogs.
He sneaks out beastly bottom-burps
and blames it on our dogs!

But despite his nasty habits,
I will always love
my naughty, cheeky, bogey-eating,
yucky little bruv!

# STRANGE PETS

My cat wears frilly knickers.
My hamster wears a bra.
They strut around my bedroom
playing drums and bass guitar.

The Funky Piglets, Volume 1

My lizard screeches on his sax
while spider toots the flute.
But they do not wear any clothes
except a bunch of fruit!

I know my pets are very strange,
as it's quite plain to see.
But I assure you that my pets
are not as strange as me!

# THE THING!

There's a "thing" in the bathroom
with green, curly toes
and a flashing red light
at the end of its nose!

The Funky Piglets, Volume 1

It has large, pointed teeth
and a wiggly bum.
But the "thing" does not scare me
'cos it's just my mum!

# SOX THE GREEDY CAT

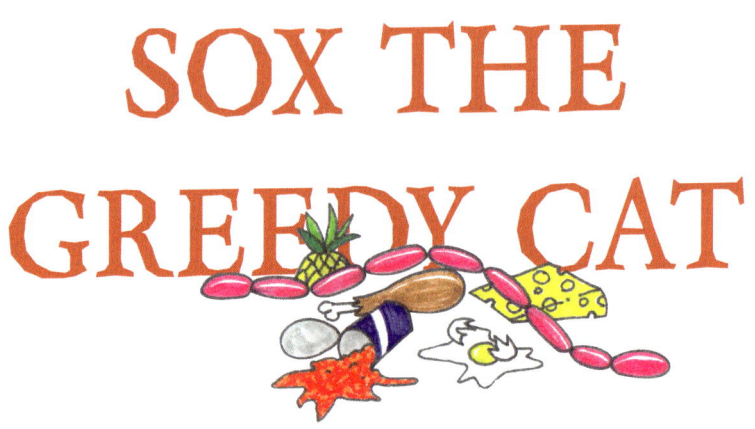

One sunny summer's evening
Sox knocked on my door.
I took him in and gave him milk
but the poor cat wanted more.

The Funky Piglets, Volume 1

So I looked inside my cupboards
for something nice to eat,
to give this hungry, ginger tom
a yummy feline treat!

I took out all the food I had
and laid it on the floor.
The famished cat scoffed everything
then asked me for some more.

The Funky Piglets, Volume 1

I told him there was nothing left.
My cupboards were quite bare.
But the greedy cat screamed, "Give me food!"
then ate the kitchen chair!

He gobbled up my table,
the sink and oven door,
the carpet, curtains and my fridge.
Yet still he begged for more!

His big, fat tum was fit to burst;
it was truly overloaded.
And so with an almighty *BANG!*
the greedy cat exploded!

Now there's Sox upon my ceiling,
my walls and kitchen floor.
Oh, how I wish I'd never let
that cat through my front door!

# WOLFGANG VON ROSE

Wolfgang von Rose
had a very strange nose.
It was two metres long
and resembled a hose.
With nostrils so
powerful,
his ginormous snout
once caused a typhoon
as a small sneeze
popped out!

The Funky Piglets, Volume 1

But Wolfgang's great conk
was a troublesome thing,
as he once discovered
while meeting the king.
For out of his snozzle
a sneeze so immense
blew out the king's teeth –
clean over the fence!

The royal policeman
arrested von Rose.
He read him his rights
and then handcuffed his nose.
Now Wolfgang's in prison
and that's all because
the poor man was born
with a super-size snozz!

# MY ANNOYING SISTER

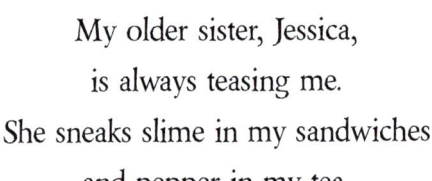

My older sister, Jessica,
is always teasing me.
She sneaks slime in my sandwiches
and pepper in my tea.

 The Funky Piglets, Volume 1

She creeps into my room at night
while I'm asleep in bed,
takes felt tips from my pencil case
and doodles on my head!

But even though she makes me cross
I wouldn't want another.
'Cos she's my super-special sis
And I'm her yucky brother!

# FUNKY PIGLETS

Funky piglets, one, two, three,
four tigers and a chimpanzee,
five elephants, six tabby cats
and seven smelly sewer rats ...

## The Funky Piglets, Volume 1

A crocodile and eight warthogs,
an eagle owl, nine snappy dogs,
ten bouncing bunnies and a mouse
have moved into my little house!

Now sadly there's no room for me.
My tiny house is full, you see.
And so the piglets moved me to
their stinky cage in Hognut Zoo!

### Message from the author, Richard Mark Smith:

I would like to thank: my partner, Rachel, for her eternal patience during the creation of *The Funky Piglets*, Volume 1; my father Gordon, mother Marlene, and sister Alyson, who, given more time, would have undoubtedly been The Funky Piglets' biggest fans; my children, Charlie and George, for their encouragement and feedback; Louise for her invaluable input and support; Catherine for creating such a wonderful book design; and Ashley for bringing my characters to life and never once, to the best of my knowledge, losing patience with me!

### Message from the illustrator, Ashley Hipperson:

I would like to say a big thank you to my family for supporting me with my art, especially my wife, Tracy, for being patient with me while I spent so many evenings drawing! And a special thank you to my little boy, Bailey, for inspiring me to draw appropriately for children! Last but not least, a big cheer to Mark for giving me this opportunity to get out my felt tips and bring his amazing characters to life in this wonderful book.

I hope you enjoy looking at my pictures.

Be sure to watch out for Sidney the sparrow – he pops up in the background on many occasions!

CPSIA information can be obtained at www.ICGtesting.com
Printed in the USA
LVIW01n1927071215
465791LV00001B/9